Welcome to the laboratory of the world!

Light is all around you when you are out of doors in the daytime: bright light streams from the golden sun, or a softer light shines through the clouds. On a showery day you may see coloured light shimmering in a rainbow.

In the night-time lights shine from a million and one places. Light bulbs glow under their lampshades, and long strip lights cast a cooler, silvery light. The pale yellow moon lights a dark sky that is studded with tiny, glittering stars.

Imagine a world that was dark all the time, a world with no sun and no day. How different everything would be! Light is part of the way the world works, and all living things depend on it.

But *why* is there light? The 'why' questions are always the hardest! The most famous book in the world, the Bible, says that in the beginning, before there was anything else in the world, God said, let there be light—and there *was* light. It was the first stage of making the entire world, and people to live in it.

Contents

1 Lights in the sky

2 Shadow shapes

3 Fun with shadows

4 Big rainbows

5 Little rainbows

6 Colour and light

7 Mirror in the sky

8 Mirror on the earth

9 Fun with mirrors

10 Night lights

11 Light for life

12 Light to see by

13 Tricks of light

14 Larger than life

1 Lights in the sky

Light! Without it, we couldn't see anything and nothing would grow.

Imagine how big the sun must be... how bright, how hot, how powerful, how much greater than anything people have ever made.

In this book you will find out some of the amazing things that light can do. You can do tests to find out for yourself that light always works in the same way.

Praise be to God for all his creatures,
and especially our brother the sun
who brings us the day and brings us the light.
How beautiful he is! How splendid!
O God, he reminds us of you.

Francis of Assisi

Does the sun really travel across the sky?

No! The sun is a blazing ball of fire, and the earth is like a spinning top that spins round it.

1 In the morning, you can see the sun on the horizon, that far-off line where the earth and sky seem to meet. It is light. It is day.

2 The sun seems to rise higher and higher in the sky.

3 Then it goes down to the horizon on the other side of the world. When it disappears, it is dark. It is night.

The Wonder of Light

by
Bonita Searle-Barnes

Illustrated by Colin Smithson

A LION BOOK
Oxford · Batavia · Sydney

Text by Bonita Searle-Barnes
Copyright © 1993 Lion
Publishing
Illustrations copyright ©
1993 Colin Smithson

Published by
Lion Publishing plc
Sandy Lane West, Oxford,
England
ISBN 0 7459 2024 1
Albatross Books Pty Ltd
PO Box 320, Sutherland,
NSW 2232, Australia
ISBN 0 7324 0507 6

First edition 1993

Acknowledgments
Photographs by Lion
Publishing: spread 14 (left);
Lion Publishing/John
Williams Studios: spreads 9
(middle and bottom), 14
(right); Nicholas Rous:
spreads 2, 11; Zefa (UK) Ltd:
cover, spreads 1, 4, 6, 7, 8, 9
(top), 10, 12

A catalogue record for this
book is available from the
British Library

Library of Congress CIP Data
applied for

Printed and bound in
Singapore

Light...
and a whole lot
more!

Children love finding out about the world they live in. This book provides loads of activities to help them find out about light. They can have hours of fun watching the way it works and noting their discoveries. In this way they will learn the basic skills of scientific research.

- *More* They can also find out about some of the ways light can be put to work in everyday technology. Exciting projects enable them to discover the fun and the satisfaction of inventing.

- *More* Throughout the ages, children, poets, artists, and some of the world's greatest scientists have thrilled to the wonder of the natural world: the detail, the design, the beauty. The photos in this book are a starting-point for discovering more. They encourage children to look for design and beauty in the everyday world around them...the pattern of stars, the colours of the rainbow, the tiny seeds that find their way through the dark earth to the light they need to grow...and help them to enjoy their world.

- *More* This book helps them, too, to find words that express the sense of excitement and joy in it all. Here is an opportunity to explore the rich heritage of poems and songs that people have written to celebrate their world. This book draws on the psalms of the Bible, which have echoed the feelings of millions throughout the centuries, and which reflect the belief that the world is not the result of chance but the creation of a wise and loving God.

- *More* There is also the question of how light makes us feel. Things seem brighter on a sunny day, a dark night can seem scary, and a small light in a dark room can be very comforting. Children will talk about these things as they do the different activities. It is a perfect opportunity to reassure them in everyday matters.

- *More* Going beyond the everyday world, you will find natural openings for talking about the symbolic use of light and darkness, which they will find in songs and stories and in a good deal of religious language. For example, the Bible speaks of Jesus as the Light of the World: bringing new life to people, and lighting their path so they can see how to live in the right way. Christians sometimes light candles to remind them of this hope. Light is used as a symbol in other religions, too. You can talk about the symbols children see around them, and explain their meaning for those who use them.

This book is intended to give a very broad approach to exploring light, that will enrich your children's total understanding of their world. You'll be surprised at what you discover, too, as you explore the world through a child's eyes.

Earth and sun model

What to do:

1 Make cuts down one end of the tube and tape it to the bottom of the ball as in the picture.

2 On the label draw a picture of a house. Put a flower on one side and a cat on the other, like this.

You will need:

- a table lamp
- a large ball
- a card tube
- scissors
- sticky tape
- a sticky label
- felt pens

4 Find a dark room where you can do this experiment. Switch on the table lamp. Turn the ball on the tube. Where does the light shine as you turn it?

From where I am on this tiny earth, I can see the light rising on the flower side and going down on the cat side.

3 Stick the label on the ball.

It shines on the flower first, then on the house, then on the sleeping cat.

The side of the earth where the sun rises is called the east.
The side of the earth where the sun sets is called the west.

2 Shadow shapes

Everything that is in the light is bright.

A shadow is a dark patch that the light can't reach because there is something in the way.

The shape of a shadow matches the outside edge of an object. Check this for yourself.

Woods are dark places because the trees get in the way of the sun's light and cast shadows around themselves. Woodland plants are designed to grow in the dim greenish light.

Simple shadows

You will need:

- a torch
- small objects such as a pencil, a key, a small toy

What to do:

1 Hold the torch so that it shines straight down on to a table in a dark room. Now put one of your objects into the light.

2 Can you see the shadow on the table? What shape is it?

3 Move the torch closer to the object. What happens to the size?

4 What happens to the size if you move it further away? What happens to the edges of the shadow?

See how it moves around when you move your torch.

Look! If I hold the torch to the side, the shadow grows longer.

Shadow clock

Outdoor shadows are best when the weather is sunny.

Find out how the shadows change as the earth turns and the sunlight shines from a different place in the sky.

You will need:

- two pencils
- cotton reel
- sticky putty
- white card

What to do:

1 Stand one pencil in the cotton reel. Use sticky putty to fix the reel to a large piece of white card.

2 Early on a sunny day, put your model outdoors or on a window-sill where the sun will shine on it. Use sticky putty to hold it in place.

3 Draw round the shadow with a pencil. Write in the time.

4 Check the shadow 1 hour later. Draw round the shadow you see now, and write in the time.

5 Do the same every hour until the end of the day. How do the shadows change?

Tomorrow I'll be able to tell the time from Bear's shadow clock.

As long as he doesn't move it. At least we can trust the sun to stay the same.

- When are they longest?
- When are they shortest?
- Watch the shadows of trees and houses during the day. Do they change like the shadows in your model?

3 Fun with shadows

Action shadows

- Can you stop someone by jumping on their shadow?
- Can you run away from your own shadow?
- Can you jump on your own shadow?
- Can your shadow shake hands with a friend's shadow if you are not touching each other?
- Look for birds flying overhead. Can you see their shadows racing over the ground?

Try jumping on her shadow. Perhaps that will stop her!

Puff

Can't catch me!

Shadow pictures

Portraits of people done like this are called silhouettes. Everyone's silhouette is different, just as people are different.

Sit still

You will need:

- large piece of white paper
- pencil
- sticky putty

What to do:

1 Find a place where the sun is shining on a wall and fix a large piece of white paper to the wall.

2 If there isn't any sunshine, use a bright torch in a dark room and let the light shine on the paper.

3 Get a friend to sit sideways-on in the light, so their shadow is on the paper.

4 Draw round the shadow.

Shadow showtime

- Move your hands and fingers to make interesting shadow shapes on a wall.

- You can make some exciting animal shapes. Try some of the ideas here.

- Put on a shadow show with your friends, making a story with different animal shadows.

4 Big rainbows

Have you ever seen a rainbow? Isn't it wonderful! All those colours make a huge arch in the sky.

Have you ever been so close to the end of a rainbow that you can see all those shimmering colours reach down to the ground?

Light simply shows us all the wonderful colours in the world around us: all the colours in the rainbow!

Hunt the rainbow

Sometimes it's raining from clouds in one part of the sky, but you can still see the sun shining in another part.

Turn so that you are facing away from the sun.

When the sunlight shines through the raindrops, it is bent by the water. The white light from the white-hot sun fans out to make a rainbow.

> Oh, is that what's happening? I think I'll just enjoy the way it looks, and the way all the colours flow into each other.

The story of the first rainbow

Do you know the story of Noah's ark? It's in the Bible. It tells how God saved a man named Noah, along with his family, and all the animals, from a great flood. When at last the flood ended, Noah saw a beautiful rainbow in the sky. God told him that the rainbow was his promise that the earth would never again be destroyed by a flood. So the next time it rained, Noah wasn't afraid: he knew that God always keeps his promises—and there was the rainbow to remind him.

5 Little rainbows

Garden rainbow

Rainbows are so lovely, it's hard to wait for the weather to be just right. But you can make your own little rainbow any time you want.

You can't touch light, and you can't touch a rainbow.

Floating rainbows

A bubble is made of a thin layer of soapy water, so clear you can see through it.

Very thin layers of clear materials can split up white light to show its rainbow colours.

What to do:

1 Blow through the straw into the bowl of soapy water to make a bubble mountain.

2 Or dip your bubble blower into the bowl and blow a floater.

3 Quick, before the bubbles go! Can you see rainbow colours on the bubble surface?

- Where else can you see rainbows?

Rainbow factory

Light can be split up into colours when it goes through clear materials such as glass or plastic.

If you hold a glass tumbler with a thick base up to the light, you may see rainbow colours.

Because light always works in this way, people have designed some things so that they will always make rainbows that are easy to see.

6 Colour and light

When there is hardly any light, you can only see grey shapes.

But in the light, you can see the world in full colour.

Look around at the colours of the world, and all the designs and patterns. What a wonderful creation it is!

> I wish I had a tail like that!

Everything you can see absorbs some of the colours in light and bounces back the others. Your eyes can pick up the colour of light that bounces back.

> And the little blue marbles are absorbing all the colours of light except blue, which bounces back.

> And I suppose the yellow marble absorbs all the colours except yellow, which bounces back.

> See how the little blue marbles went through the arches, but the big yellow one bounced back. You can still see it, here.

Colour change

Some types of light don't have all the colours that are in sunlight. Objects can't bounce back colours that aren't already in the light that shines on them, so the objects themselves may look different. Find out for yourself.

You will need:

- torch
- coloured sweet paper

What to do:

1 Shine the torch on something white. What colour is it?

2 Now put the coloured sweet paper over the torch and shine it on something white. What colour does it look now?

3 Shine your torch on different coloured things. Do they all look the same colour as they do in sunlight? If not, what colour do they become? Make a list.

The light was coloured...	I shone it on...	It looked...
red	a yellow ball	orange
red	a blue ball	

▶ 7 Mirror in the sky

The moon has no light of its own, but on a clear night you can see it as a soft, silvery light.

The moon is a ball of rock that travels around the earth. Its journey takes 28 days. It seems to shine because it reflects light from the sun to the earth.

What a good design for a natural night-light!

Bedroom moon

You will need:

- balloon
- kitchen foil
- string

What to do:

1 Blow up the balloon.

2 Wrap it in kitchen foil.

3 Attach a piece of string and hang it in your bedroom. The foil will reflect back any light that shines on it.

- If the light comes from one direction you will see moon shapes of light.

Watching the moon

1 Watch the sky each night for a month.

2 Each night, draw a picture of the moon, if you can see it. Copy its shape exactly.

3 Don't forget to draw clouds instead if the sky is cloudy!

● What happens to the size and shape of the moon?

> You need to remember every night if you want good results!

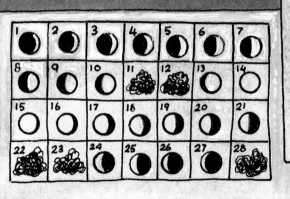

An evening prayer

Are you afraid of the dark? For hundreds of years people who trusted God have said a prayer like this at evening time:

> *When I lie down*
> *I sleep in peace*
> *For only God*
> *Can keep me safe.*
>
> **From Psalm 4 of the Bible**

8 Mirror on the earth

Smooth, shiny surfaces bounce light back. They act as mirrors, reflecting a picture back to you.

Clear, still water is a natural mirror.

Hunt the mirror

How many things can you find in which you can see your reflection?

Don't get your feet wet!

I can see myself, but the reflection is dark like the foil.

I don't think this one's shiny enough.

Upside-down world

You will need:

- a small, flat mirror
- stiff paper or thin card
- crayons
- sticky tape
- scissors
- coloured modelling dough

What to do:

1 Lay the mirror flat.

2 Measure a piece of paper long enough to go round the edge of the mirror. Now lay it flat and draw a lakeside picture, with trees bending their branches down, rushes, and bright yellow water plants and all the animals and birds that you can think of that live by the water.

3 Now cut out the top edge of your picture.

4 Then tape it into a circle and stand it up on your mirror. Can you see the reflection of your world in the mirror lake?

5 Make some ducks out of modelling dough, and put them on the lake to swim.

9 Fun with mirrors

This is a bad mirror. I've put my badge on the left, and the mirror's put my badge on the right.

Mirrors don't muddle things, they just bounce light back.

That's why the bounced picture gets the right on the left.

The results can be quite a surprise.

Working backwards

Once you understand how a mirror picture works, you can use it in different ways.

to see the back of your head

to see behind you

to see in awkward places

Double, double

You will need:

- a small flat mirror

Make a whole butterfly. Can you make it flutter its wings?

Put your mirror on this line. Is the mirror leaf the same as the whole leaf? Can you work out why?

Give this daisy its petals back!

▶ 10 Night lights

At night time, you can often see lots of stars.

A star is a sun, but much further away than our sun—millions of kilometres away. Starlight can take millions of years to reach us, travelling all that distance.

The nearest star to us is called Sirius. Its light has to travel for 9 years before it reaches the Earth.

There are millions of stars in our part of the universe. A collection of stars is called a galaxy, and our galaxy is called the Milky Way. It looks like a whorl of twinkling diamonds.

The universe must be ENORMOUS. And everything works in its own way, from faraway stars that light our night-time to the tiniest, tiniest plants and animals. There must be a mastermind behind it.

When I look at the sky, which you have made
And the moon and the stars you put there
I wonder why you take the time
To think of someone as small as me.

From Psalm 8 of the Bible

Nightlight

The sun and stars are huge balls of fire. For thousands of years, people have made tiny fires to light the night-time.

Fire can be very dangerous. You will need a grown-up to be your scientific assistant.

A torch is safer. Never go away and leave your candle burning.

You will need:

- a glass jar
- a small candle
- some matches
- water

What to do:

1 Ask your grown-up assistant to light the candle. As the wax around the flame melts, ask them to drip some into the jar, and then stand the candle upright in the wax. Wait till the wax hardens again.

2 Now add about 2cm water to the jar.

3 Next, ask your grown-up assistant to light the candle. It gives off a little point of light that can be very comforting in the dark.

- The water helps weight the jar so it doesn't tip easily. If it is tipped the water will help put the flame out. If the candle is left burning, the flame will go out when it reaches the water.

- What happens if you hold a mirror behind the flame? Does it make the light seem brighter?

- What happens to the flame if your grown-up assistant puts a lid on the jar?

Light in the darkness

A light helps you to find your way in the darkness.

People sometimes speak of other things that are like a light, helping them to find their way through life. These lines are from the Bible.

The people who live as God wants,
Who are kind, and fair, and forgiving,
Are like people with light in the darkness.
And they are happy.

From Psalm 112 of the Bible

11 Light for life

Have you noticed how fast plants grow in summer? Sometimes they grow so fast that you can find new young leaves every day.

Yesterday it had six. Today it's got eight.

Plants grow fastest when the days are long, because they use the sunlight to make food for themselves in their leaves.

Plants are designed to catch as much light as possible. Sunflowers actually turn towards the sun.

The escaping bean

Test to see if your bean can find its way to the light.

You will need:

- small pot of soil
- bean seed
- water
- cardboard box
- scissors

What to do:

1 Plant the bean seed in the soil and water it well.

2 Put the pot in the box and close it. Poke a hole in the side with the scissors.

3 Leave it in a warm place and check the soil every day to make sure it is still damp.

4 See if your bean can find its way to the light.

Cress experiment

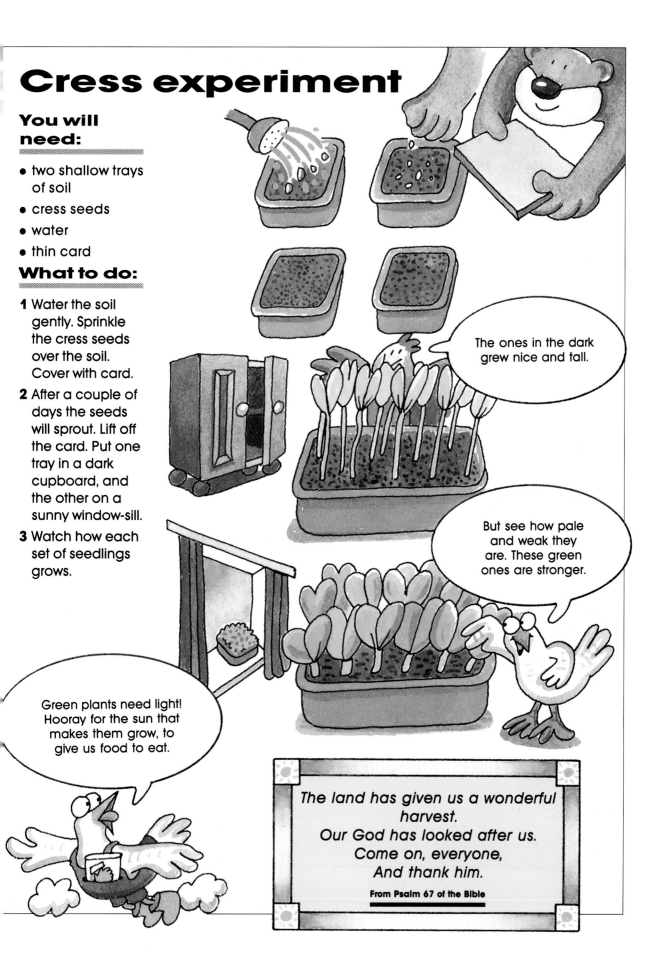

You will need:

- two shallow trays of soil
- cress seeds
- water
- thin card

What to do:

1 Water the soil gently. Sprinkle the cress seeds over the soil. Cover with card.

2 After a couple of days the seeds will sprout. Lift off the card. Put one tray in a dark cupboard, and the other on a sunny window-sill.

3 Watch how each set of seedlings grows.

The ones in the dark grew nice and tall.

But see how pale and weak they are. These green ones are stronger.

Green plants need light! Hooray for the sun that makes them grow, to give us food to eat.

The land has given us a wonderful harvest.
Our God has looked after us.
Come on, everyone,
And thank him.

From Psalm 67 of the Bible

▶ 12 Light to see by

You need light to see things.

But the light doesn't have to be bright. You can see something in a dim light, because your eyes are specially designed to open up and let more light in.

They close up more when the light is bright.

The part of the eye that lets in the light is the dark part in the centre, called the pupil.

Wide eyes

Some animals can see very well in the dark. Have a look at these pictures. Why do you think they can see so well?

Intelligent eyes

- Look in a mirror at your eyes. Notice the dark part in the centre.
- Now go into a place that is brightly lit— perhaps outdoors, if it is sunny.
- After a few minutes, look at your eyes again. Have your pupils changed size?
- Now go into a dark place, such as a walk-in cupboard, for a few minutes.
- Now look at your eyes again. What has happened to your pupils now?

Make sure someone knows you're there!

Cool shades

The Inuit people of North America invented shades like these to protect their eyes from the dazzle of the snow. The tiny holes in them let very little light shine in your eyes.

You will need:

- a piece of thin card
- scissors
- felt pen
- a toothpick

What to do:

1 Cut the card to make a band that goes over your eyes, with a bit cut away for your nose, and curved ends to go over your ears.

2 Put the shades on. With the felt pen gently mark two spots on the card, one over the middle of each eye. DON'T POKE.

3 Take the shades off and poke holes through the marks with the toothpick.

4 Now try them on!

13 Tricks of light

Light always works in the same way.

But it behaves one way in the air, and another way in water.

Look carefully at what it does in water. You may be surprised!

The broken pencil

You will need:

- a glass tumbler
- a pencil

What to do:

1 Fill a glass tumbler half fall of water and put a pencil in it.

2 Look from the top. What can you see?

3 Now look from the side.

Whose feet?

Next time you go paddling, in the bath or in a pool, look at your feet.

Do they look the same as usual? What is different?

Water ceiling

You will need:

- a glass tumbler
- water
- a toy that floats
- a strip of paper

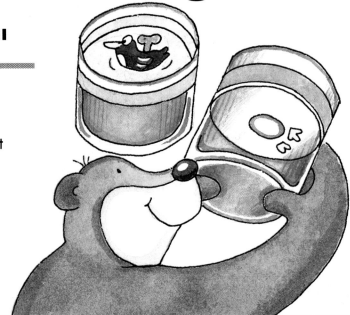

What to do:

1 Put some water in a glass tumbler and float a small toy on top. Wrap a piece of paper round the tumbler at the water line.

2 Look through the sides of the tumbler. Can you see the part of your toy that is above water?

3 Now look through the bottom. Can you see out through the water now?

Top half, bottom half

This is the view from the glass side of a pond at the zoo.
Can you match the feet to the bird?

▶ 14 Larger than life

The way light bends in water can make objects look larger than they really are.

Raindrops can have this effect. Next time it has been raining, have a look at a leaf with a raindrop on it.

If the drop is the right shape, it will make the details of the leaf underneath it seem larger

Look at the tiny details on this leaf. With a magnifying glass, you can discover a whole new world.

Magnifying glass

Make a water magnifying glass.

You will need:

- foil bottle top, or piece of foil cut from a freezer container
- wooden skewer
- water
- newspaper

I can see everything bigger than ever.

What to do:

1 Make a hole in the piece of foil with the skewer.

2 With your finger, put a drop of water on the hole, so it fills it like a tiny window pane.

3 Lift the foil carefully to your eye and look through the water at the newspaper. What do you see?

- What is the shape of the water drop that works?

- What happens if you make the hole larger?

I spy

A glass or plastic magnifying glass has a curved shape like a water drop.

- Collect some natural objects from the garden or from a walk, such as leaves, twigs, flowers and seed heads.
- Look at them carefully with a magnifying glass and draw what you can see.

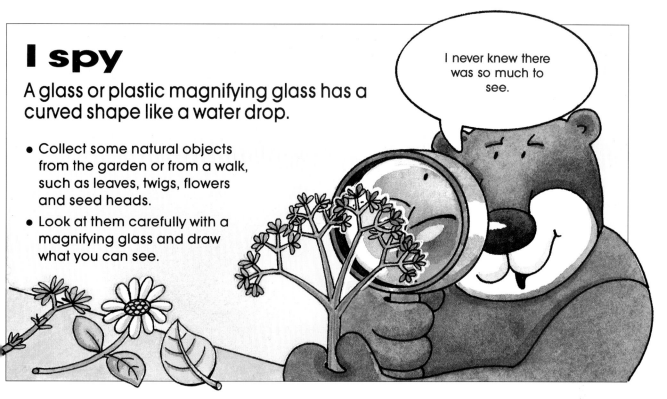

Nature detective

Here are some natural objects several times larger than they really are. Can you work out what they are?

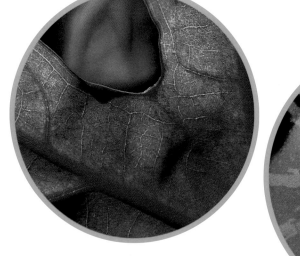

- Be careful not to leave a magnifying glass around! It bends the sun's rays to make the ground underneath extra hot. This can even start a fire, and spoil precious woods and countryside.

The skies above us show how wonderful God is
And the marvellous things he has done.
Each day tells the next day,
Each night tells the next night.
You will not hear their voice,
But what they say is clear to all the world.

From Psalm 19 of the Bible